Mystical South Carolina

A Pilgrimage to Joy

By Teri Leigh Teed

MYSTICAL SOUTH CAROLINA - A PILGRIMAGE TO JOY
Copyright © 2019 Teri Leigh Teed. All rights reserved.

First Edition: October 2019

No part of this book may be reproduced or transmitted in any form or by any means, electronic or mechanical, including photography, recording or any information storage and retrieval system, without written permission from the author and publisher.

Published by: Teri Leigh Teed Healing Spirit Art Press
               P. O. Box 731
               Dillsboro, NC 28725

ISBN: 978-1-7331739-0-2

www.terileighteed.com

Cover photo: Reflections on Black Creek
Interior book design: My House of Design
Editor: Donna Glee Williams
Author photo: Terri Clark Photography

*Dedicated
To Mom, with love*

Table of Contents

Foreword 1
What Is a Pilgrimage? 7
Chapter 1 Healing Springs: Angelic Encounters 11
Chapter 2 Cathedral of Highway 3: Encounter with Light 17
Chapter 3 Congaree Swamp: Earth Beams and Black Panthers 23
Chapter 4 Blair: The Ferry/Faery Crossing 29
Chapter 5 Lake Monticello: The Spirit of the Lake 35
Chapter 6 The Singing Trees of 601: Heaven and Nature 41
Chapter 7 Landsford Canal: The Language of Flowers 45
Chapter 8 Old Sheldon Church: The Stonehenge of the South 51
Chapter 9 Lutheran Theological Southern Seminary: Walking the Labyrinth . . . 57
Chapter 10 Middleton Place: The Labyrinth in the Rice Fields 63
Chapter 11 Pearl Fryar's Topiary Garden: Love, Peace and Goodwill 69
Chapter 12 Kalmia Gardens: The Divine Feminine Presence 77
Postscript 83
The Congaree Rings 89
The Twelve Sacred Sites 93
Acknowledgments 97
Resources 99
My Passport to the Twelve Sacred Sites 108
About the Author 111

Circular Water

Foreword

"A pilgrimage is a very personal journey that gives us the space to experience our soul."

What would you do if you were not afraid? What mystical journey would you undertake? If you are ready to step out on your own pilgrimage in life, these pages were written for you.

This book was born shortly after I moved back to my hometown of Columbia, South Carolina, in late 2004. At the time, I was not really happy to be back in my birthplace. Coming home felt like admitting defeat, going back to the beginning again, starting over at Square One. To help you understand why, here's a little of my story.

In August 1999, I'd left a satisfying, interesting job as the executive in charge of Kentucky Derby tickets at Churchill Downs in Louisville, Kentucky, where I'd worked for more than ten years. I withdrew my life savings and moved to London on my own to study art history at Sotheby's Institute of Art for one year.

That one-year plan turned into a two-year adventure as I worked for Queen Elizabeth at Buckingham Palace, lived in pastoral Ireland outside Dublin for three months while studying for my finals, and completed a master's degree in Decorative Arts and Historic Interiors from the University of Buckingham.

After returning to the United States, I sold my house in Louisville, started my own antiques consulting business, and moved back home to South Carolina. While starting my new business, I lived with my mom in her home in Manning. I am so grateful for the time we spent together before her death, traveling around South Carolina and Western North Carolina looking for antiques.

My travel adventures continued during those years. I went back to England to sample antiques fairs. I attended the famed Ashes cricket match in Sydney, Australia, as a guest writer. I spent a month housesitting a fifteenth-century chateau in the heart of France, looking for antiques, keeping a journal, and taking photographs of daily scenes, as well as other chateaus including Chenonceau, Blois, and Chambord.

Mom had a wonderful library rich with books on a variety of topics. A volume on crystal healing piqued my interest and became the seed that germinated into the book you are holding in your hands today. Her library gave context to what I'd experienced as

I'd traveled abroad and visited venerated places like Stonehenge in England, Notre Dame Cathedral in France, the Alhambra in Spain, and Glendalough in Ireland. Sacred sites, sacred travels—they stirred something in my soul.

But do sacred sites always have to be half a world away? Did coming home to South Carolina have to mean my days of pilgrimage were over?

When I moved back to Columbia in late 2004 and got my own apartment, to lift my spirits I decided to find out more about sacred spaces in the state where I'd started my journey on this Earth. But I couldn't find any books about the subject. None. So I started making my own notes. I explored. I followed vague leads to places I'd never been, never heard of. I kept journals. I wandered and I wondered. I took photographs. Eventually, like atoms organizing into a crystal, these thoughts and travels became this book.

The first place on my pilgrimage was Healing Springs. An easy hour's drive from the capital city of Columbia, that first visit sparked a wildfire in my heart. And so my sojourn began, and through personal and business travels over the next seven years, this new path took me throughout my home state and opened my mind to the other realms of our daily existence. And brought me peace of mind and joy.

Pilgrimages need not be limited to far away places after all. On this homegrown, Deep South pilgrimage of mine, I found out about myself. I learned that, like pebbles tossed in a pond, we make many circles in life. And our own circles overlap with other's circles along the way to form a magnificent, all-connected web of humanity and Nature.

This book is intended to be a starting point. It is by no means all-inclusive, as there are many other wonderful places to explore in this beautiful state. And that's part of the path to joy—finding your own sacred spaces and creating your own new experiences.

Leave your GPS behind and use your own inner compass, your intuition, to guide you. On this trip, it's okay to get lost. That's when you get to stop, ask directions, and meet new friends. When you find yourself on sacred ground, thank the spirits of the places you visit, tread lightly there, and keep an open mind. Above all, allow yourself to have fun!

My sincere wish is for you to travel to these places and open your heart and soul for your own mystical experiences. Share them with your families and friends. Remember, all roads lead us home. Happy travels!

Namaste,

Teri Leigh Teed

*"When you feel a peaceful joy,
that is when you are near truth."
~ Rumi (1207-1273)*

The Road to Mayfair Plantation

What Is a Pilgrimage?

"Travel is more than the seeing of sights; it is a change that goes on, deep and permanent, in the ideas of living."
~ Miriam Beard (1876-1958)

We each come into this world whole, knowing all deep inside ourselves. As we grow up, the bruising barrage of socialization, conventional education, and family wounds knock us out of contact with our original wholeness. Hungry for healing, we spend our lives remembering and reconnecting with our souls and our life mission, our unique role to play upon this Earth. A pilgrimage is a very personal journey that gives us the space to experience our soul.

Traditionally, pilgrimage involves travel through physical space, whether that be the five hundred miles of the Camino de Santiago or the forty-two feet of the Labyrinth at Chartres. Travel invites new experiences and enlightening moments. Changes in scenery change our perspective. Taking a back road instead of a highway leads us to new vistas and a more relaxed pace. Slowing down relaxes and renews our bodies, minds, and spirits, opening us to a more thoughtful receptivity to the lessons that come our way. How we view our world is shaped by our beliefs and, in the press of ordinary "reality," often all we see is what we believe. Travel challenges our preconceptions. It leads us to grapple with what's really there.

When we travel, we unavoidably move through Nature, which is an integral part of our path to wholeness. Meeting and experiencing our interconnectedness with all things is like a mirror that offers us back knowledge about who we really are.

On my own journeys, peering through a camera at that mirror has been a vital part of the pilgrimage. When I first moved back to my hometown, photography brought me to many new places in my home state. I might not have ever known that Albert Einstein once visited a local home in a neighboring county had I not taken the opportunity to see through the camera's lens. For you it may be something different. Maybe the novelty and relaxation of pilgrimage will invite you to sit and journal in a place that calls your heart. Maybe you will take the time to draw a picture of a luminous discovery. Maybe you will stretch your limbs and move your body to dance with the spirit of a sacred space. Take a chance today. Open your heart, be a pilgrim, and change your world.

Who knows what you will find?

> *"One's destination is never a place,*
> *but a new way of seeing things."*
> *~ Henry Miller (1891-1980)*

Mystical South Carolina

Healing Springs

1

Healing Springs: Angelic Encounters

"Hope springs eternal..."
~ Alexander Pope (1688-1744)

In the summer of 2005, my intuition prompted me to research the locations of natural springs in South Carolina. I discovered that Healing Springs was just an hour's drive from Columbia and I suggested to my mother and brother that we visit this oasis together during his vacation that July. We packed a picnic and set out for the little town of Blackville, South Carolina, just three miles south of Healing Springs.

Stories tell of four British loyalists who were critically injured in a Revolutionary War battle less than a mile away from the springs on Windy Hill Creek. The wounded men were left behind with two fellow soldiers instructed to bury them when they died. But fortune smiled on them and they were rescued by compassionate Native Americans who helped them to the nearby springs, long revered by indigenous people who believed the water had healing properties, a gift from the Great Spirit. After partaking of the spring waters for several months, the wounded soldiers fully recovered and returned to their commander in Charleston, much to the amazement of their comrades-in-arms.

Once, when I was living in a cottage in Camden, about an hour and a half from Healing Springs, I was awakened one night by spirits of departed British soldiers from the Revolutionary War. I asked them what they wanted, and they replied to "go home." So I envisioned a boat to take them down the Wateree River and on to Charleston and then England, and off they went. I have since wondered if the soldiers who returned to Charleston from Healing Springs were sent up to Camden.

Since my first visit, I have returned to Healing Springs often, sometimes with friends and sometimes solo, always with a car full of empty plastic milk jugs or other containers to fill with the spring water and then take home to enjoy and share with family and friends.

On one occasion I delivered some water from Healing Springs to my mom at her home in Manning and left an extra jug for her neighbor, who was ecstatically grateful. It turned out that he grew up near Healing Springs and often visited his uncle and grandfather who lived there. He'd learned to swim in a small canal there, encircled by a rubber tire inner tube and pulled by a mule walking along the bank, with his uncle gently holding the reins and giving encouragement to his nephew.

Today Healing Springs still flows freely. In the 1940s, one acre of this land was deeded to God for public use, giving it its nickname "God's Acre." Visitors come daily from all over to drink the healing waters in the shade of majestic trees, in the shadow of an 18th century chapel, surrounded by angels, visible and invisible. Two angel statues stand vigil in a front yard just down the street from the springs.

On one of my trips, there were people waiting in line at the metal water taps installed to make access to the wonderful spring water easier. I was filling my water containers when a well-dressed gentleman in a business suit arrived. He removed his jacket and left it in his polished imported car, and walked up calmly and stood by Windy Hill Creek, the small stream running by the springs at the edge of the swamp, serenely waiting his turn for an available tap.

I spoke to this tall, elegant, quiet gentleman and invited him to use the available taps in the area where I was filling my containers. He thanked me politely and proceeded to fill a very large, stadium-size plastic container with the soothing water.

He finished filling his container before I'd filled all of mine, and turned to thank me again before he lifted his huge, heavy container of water to take to his car.

"Thank you for sharing your space with me today," he said softly in a deep voice with a gracious and humble smile. He walked reverently toward his car, placed the container inside and then drove slowly away. Immediately a chill ran up my spine, as if some ancient recognition had taken place. There was an aura of peace and tranquility about him that complemented the spirit of Healing Springs and amplified it in a gentle and caring way.

I pondered on this unique encounter all the way home, and it occurred to me I knew exactly whom I had met—an angel.

When you visit God's Acre, remember to give thanks to the spirit of this lovely place, and the essence of Healing Springs will fill you with peace, along with its sparkling clear, cool, delicious water.

And if taking photographs, consider experimenting with the sepia or black and white setting on your digital camera and see if anything remarkable appears in your photos.

It is my profound belief that there are many mystical places on our wonderful planet that possess the power to heal, to reconnect us to our right balance—physically, emotionally, and spiritually. Sometimes something as ordinary as water, taken and shared in the right spirit, can fling open the possibilities that surround us. We need only to open our hearts and minds, and our eyes will find them.

"Be not forgetful to entertain strangers: for thereby some have entertained angels unawares."
~ Hebrews 13:2

Mystical South Carolina

Cathedral

2

Cathedral of Highway 3: Encounter with Light

"Out beyond ideas of wrong-doing and right-doing, there is a field. I will meet you there."
~ Rumi (1207-1273)

One of the advantages of living in a state with lots of rural communities is the opportunity to choose scenic byways instead of superhighways when you travel. Along with Nature's beauty, you can also discover human-made curiosities like flea markets and roadside stands selling local fruits and vegetables and home-made crafts. In addition to old mom-and-pop establishments adorned with unique, now-faded advertising signs, you will come upon new stores sprouting along country roads as creative people find their place in the ancient landscapes. One South Carolina artist, Jim Harrison of Denmark, South Carolina, (only an hour's drive from both Columbia and

Charleston) built a large, loyal following for his paintings of the kinds of scenes you will still find along rural Southern routes: barns, beaches, country stores, and old-style cola signs.

As you wander the landscape, you will find that each community has a distinct flavor and feel, and the roads usually run alongside a railroad track or river, following the natural, easy flow of the land. One never knows what is just around the bend.

Tuning your ear to both wild and cultivated sacred sweetness requires the discipline of slow travel and the ability to pause. As you pass each crossroad, stop and ponder. Who else has passed this way? Can you reach out with your intuition to know what has happened in this place in days gone by? Are you any different from the people who lived before you and traveled this same road?

I am forever grateful to my friend Bob Medlock for his long, leisurely, chauffeured drives through the Carolina countryside with his carload full of friends. Bob introduced me to Miller's Bread Basket, a delightfully charming Amish/Mennonite family-run restaurant in the tiny hamlet of Blackville, just minutes from Healing Springs. Miller's has been serving up delicious traditional meals—think fried chicken and shoo-fly pie—since 1987, with the deep hospitality that overflows from abundant spirit.

The original Mr. Miller has retired now and so the ownership has passed into the hands of Mervin and Anna Miller, and loyal customers return like homing pigeons to this quaint and refreshing diner, a modern-day caravanserai on the pilgrim path to Healing Springs.

One Saturday afternoon, on the way back to Columbia after lingering over lunch at Miller's with Bob, the sun's rays filtered softly down a row of precision-planted pine trees across from a hayfield on Highway 3. Like the sunlight streaming through a stained glass church window, the light transported me to another place and time. It took me back to another pilgrimage I'd made so many times: the route to visit my mom along old Highway 261, a long stretch of quiet road from Highway 378 to Manning, passing through the villages of Wedgefield, Pinewood, and Paxville. Once a Native American forest path, the way was widened in 1753 into The Great Charleston Road, and is now surrounded by pine trees, fields, and the Manchester Forest. On one side of the road is a grove of pine trees planted in ruler-straight rows, similar to the one I saw that day on Highway 3, only that grove had been planted by my mother and the Women's Club she chaired in the 1960s.

Bob sensed how touched I was by the light that day—the beauty and the memories—and exercised the art of pilgrimage by pausing. He graciously turned his car around and let me stop and photograph this natural cathedral.

Through humanity's scientific explorations, we are rediscovering what Nature knows and lives every day. When we slow down and take the time to see with our hearts, Nature shows us the God within, and inspires us with her wisdom and beauty.

Slow sojourns in the South can carry our spirits high and deep into the spiritual landscape, just as much as the hikes of John Muir and the ancient pilgrim paths between the cathedrals in Europe.

They can make us look at pine trees in a whole new light.

"Believing is seeing."
~ Author unknown

Mystical South Carolina

Earth Beam

3

Congaree Swamp: Earth Beams and Black Panthers

*"Come join us in the living treetops,
where the winds of spirit blow wild and free."*
~ Ken Carey (d. 2017)

Located just twenty miles south of the capital city of Columbia, across from the bluffs of the Congaree River, the 26,000-acre Congaree National Park attracts pilgrims from all over the world. Indeed, she is probably more known and visited by people from outside South Carolina than by the residents of the state. The Congaree Swamp acts as the heart of South Carolina, circulating the waters of compassion, love, and kindness to us all as she floods and drains.

The heart chakra, one of seven energy centers of our bodies, is the bridge between the physical and spiritual worlds. The heart is one of three minds in our physical bodies: our brain, our heart, and our gut.

When we have both hemispheres in our brain working in harmony, then we are more open to our intuition, the knowledge we feel in our gut. And when we "see" with our heart, we can feel euphoria, like when we fall in love. The color green is associated with the heart chakra, and with swamps.

Have you ever wondered why we feel so peaceful when we stand in such natural wonders as the Congaree Swamp or a beach by the ocean? In the arms of Mother Nature, when we allow Her sounds and rhythms and light to permeate our bodies, our rhythms begin to match Hers. We feel at home—we can relax. When we relax, wonderful healing can take place in our physical bodies. We allow ourselves to renew and regenerate, which is what our bodies are designed to do.

In late 2005, my beloved cat Runner passed away and I discovered Congaree Swamp while processing my grief over his death. Just as this wetland filters the wastes from rivers and watersheds, the sheltering spirit of the Congaree Swamp took my sorrows and held them for me, washed me clean, and helped me heal.

A mysterious and enchanting place, locals at a nearby restaurant and church tell tales of elusive black panthers there. You can sign up for free guided night tours in the fall and winter months, which I highly recommend. Park rangers hold evening walks and call out to the owls, who return their hoot-hoots and whoosh unseen over the heads of visitors in the cold, inky night.

According to the book *Animal Speak*, by Ted Andrews, marshes and swamps are known in the spiritual community as "between-places," gateways to Great Spirit, home to fairies and Nature spirits. In summer, the Congaree Swamp is alive with the fairy-light of fireflies illuminating the night with their synchronized flashings.

It must have been amazing to have lived in America before European settlers arrived and began cutting down the ancient forests. Hosting both the tallest and the largest loblolly pines still alive today, as well as cypress trees over five hundred years old, Congaree gives us a glimpse what those old-growth forests must have been like. It is a great place to hug a tree – if you mind the poison ivy that looks like rope wrapped around it!

My favorite times to visit here are in late autumn and winter when cooler temperatures keep the "mosquito-meter" at the Welcome Center near zero. The light filters down through the tightly-woven branches and reflects softly in the brackish waters. Walking the boardwalks or pathways and canoeing the creeks is free. Soft rains and the sightings of deer and other small creatures are an added bonus. My favorite photograph created here is of an Earth Beam, a rare and unique display of seven rays of multicolored light springing up from the Earth, illuminating space and time.

The beauty of this place inspires reverence and respect. Like entering a house of worship, stepping into the Congaree Swamp invites you to still your body and mind, and allow her spirit to permeate your being. Water, the giver of life, is the conduit, and our thoughts, intentions, and prayers are the energies the Congaree soaks up and filters, then returns to us renewed. Isn't that what a sacred space is meant to be? Match your rhythms to her pulse, and see how it feels.

All the Congaree Swamp asks of you is to keep her safe and allow her to live freely and do what she is designed for.

"Life is a gift of nature; but beautiful living is the gift of wisdom."
~ Greek adage

Mystical South Carolina

Old Barn, Blair

4

Blair:
The Ferry/Faery Crossing

*"As a river is born deep inside the earth in springs
that gather into streams and join to become a river,
so do people's lives gather into families and communities
and become part of the river of history."*
~ Wilma Dykeman (1920-2006)

In 2005, I met a local photographer who introduced me to Blair. A sleepy hamlet of about 1,500 souls in Fairfield County, Blair was once a bustling center of the local economy, hosting both the commercially important ferry crossing and the general store. Located midway between the charming towns of Winnsboro and Newberry on Highway 34, Blair is a lovely stop on a quiet drive through wooded countryside.

When I first visited Blair, the general store was still open on Saturdays as an antique shop, and locals swapped stories there as the proprietor offered free coffee and colas to visitors, along with homemade, freshly cooked sausage from a cast iron skillet.

Looking at old maps, so easy in these days of online archives, is a favorite way of mine to get a feel for how areas have evolved over the centuries. One can see how some of our roads follow the old Native American forest paths, which in turn followed the animal trails. I feel different when I travel an old, historic back road instead of an interstate highway; do you? I am intrigued by the route railroads follow—are the tracks on the east, west, north, or south side of a river, and why? Old maps are a way into the history of the landscape; they are the "scriptures" of the spirit of place.

Named Fairfield by the British for the tranquil rolling hills and vistas, perhaps reminding them of the Cotswolds, the area around Blair was originally home to the trails used by the Catawba and the Cherokee. The old names of its roadways reflect this, as Highway 215 was known as "Old Cherokee Road" and Highway 34 as "Catawba Trail." The Old Wagon Road of Colonial days passes nearby, just over the Kershaw County line.

The banks of the Broad River lie just over the railroad tracks and down the hill behind the general store. Wagons filled with cotton and corn no longer cross by the ferry, but if you are quiet and in harmony with the land while you sit and listen to the Broad River's lullaby as she passes by the leafy boughs of her tree-lined banks, you may feel the presence of faeries still, and perhaps sense a portal opening between this world and the Other.

Mystical South Carolina

I was fortunate to sense one of these portals. In the mid-afternoon on a sunny spring day, I was walking along the shady ferry road by the river and all of a sudden I felt light-headed and stopped to check my balance. For a brief few moments the air seemed to sparkle and it felt as if time was suspended. There was a peaceful, joyful feeling of happy anticipation. And then it was gone.

On the bluff above the crossing, the private retreat at #1 Broad River still hosts family and friends with a view up the Broad River and the surrounding Sumter National Forest. This peaceful village is also home to Blair Art Studio, a school and gallery headed by world-famous airbrush painter extraordinaire Dru Blair, well known for his photorealistic military jet paintings celebrating "freedom through strength."

Visiting Blair and the surrounding countryside helped to open my photographic eyes at a time when I was being pounded by grief. The passing of my childhood best friend's parents and the end of a romantic relationship nearly brought me to my knees. My cat Runner died and my other cat, Mr. Scooty, missed his lifelong companion so much that he just stopped eating one day. One of his comforts during this trial was listening to the audiobook *Autobiography of a Yogi*, the story of Yogananda Paramahansa. Scooty seemed to enjoy the sound of Ben Kingsley's voice as he read, but it didn't hold him here. Two weeks later, Mr. Scooty followed Runner over the Rainbow Bridge.

My landlord had a new wooden fence erected around the Charleston-style garden outside my apartment's front door and he planted ten Rose of Sharon bushes lining the walk to the entrance. One rose bush died and nine remained. I buried Scooty's body in the place where the one rose bush had perished, across the garden path from his feline friend.

After losing both of my kitties within a short time span, I needed some uplifting energy. Badly. I started to take yoga classes. I studied more about crystal healing and ley lines, the Earth's invisible veins and arteries. I met my friend, Susan Grey, a distance healer based in Columbia with a worldwide clientele. My sorrow was softened by taking my camera and traveling the quiet country lanes in my vintage car, a 1981 Mercedes-Benz 300 CD Diesel Coupe named "Ms. Grace."

And then something led me to print some of my photographs. My landlord saw them one day. "Hon," he said in his slow drawl, "you've got a real gift." I'd never thought about selling my photographs until he said that. "Angels unawares," again.

On a whim, I visited Blair with my friend and fellow photographer, Jim, and showed the owner of the general store there several of my framed photos of the town. He purchased all of them on the spot, from the trunk of my car.

I immediately tithed to Spirit by taking Jim and another fellow photographer to dinner to celebrate.

Just looking—really looking—at the landscape and letting in the beauty and feeling of the place can help bring a shift in awareness, in our consciousness. In our life.

"A self that goes on changing is a self that goes on living."
~ Virginia Woolf (1882-1941)

Mystical South Carolina

Spirit of the Lake

5

Lake Monticello: The Spirit of the Lake

"They both listened silently to the water, which to them was not just water, but the voice of life, the voice of Being, the voice of perpetual Becoming."
~ *Hermann Hesse (1877-1962)*

Water, the basis of life on our planet, determines where people, animals, and plants take root. Indeed, in humanity's exploration of our universe, water is critical in the search for another planet on which we might reside. Sacred sites are often oriented towards water: at natural springs, on the shores of the sea, on the banks of rivers, or beside still lakes.

Just ten miles southeast of Blair you will find Lake Monticello, a man-made reservoir off the Broad River, created in 1978 to supply hydroelectric power and cool the Virgil C. Summer Nuclear

Generating Station in Jenkinsville. A boat launch and park on Highway 215 offer access. Jet skis and waterskiing are prohibited on the lake, so her quiet, clear waters and sandy beaches offer a peaceful respite from the noisy world.

One of the many photographs I have taken at Lake Monticello is one that looks beneath the surface of the clear water near the edge. Near the boat ramp there are some man-made blocks that are visible in the lake.

When I snapped this shot, it reminded me of the stories of the ancient civilization Atlantis. And so that is what I named it: "Atlantis of the South."

There is so much to our human experience that is "just under the surface," waiting for our exploration. Science tells us that we have two hemispheres in our brain in our head and both a conscious and subconscious reality. Tradition tells us that our bodies have three "brains": one in our head, one in our heart, and one in our gut. Each of these facets of the self has its own unique way of processing information. Why would anyone want to just waterski across the surface of things?

In 2007, I was diving deep, studying Celtic and Native American traditions along with natural medicines. My homeopathic veterinarian introduced me to flower essences made at Green Hope Farms in New Hampshire. I read spiritual and self-help books by Carol Tuttle, Masaru Emoto, and many other like-minded authors. I explored non-conventional treatments like Reiki and voice remapping, continuing my quest for wholeness of mind, body, and spirit. As I continued to heal myself, my creativity increased and my self-confidence soared. I learned that, to be a free and sovereign individual, you need to know your own compass, your own True North. This means freeing yourself of your own subconscious beliefs and those imposed on you from the outside by other people's projections. Relationships that no longer served my highest good began to drop away, and new opportunities presented themselves. No compass can tell you the truth when it's being pushed and tugged by outside influences.

Helping others had always been one of my personal guidelines. I'd seen the path of service demonstrated by my parents and their parents before them. What I was learning now, through my seeking, was that we must also help and heal ourselves. But how, I wondered? What was the right treatment, the right path for me? How could I balance the inflow of self-nurture with the outflow of offering my gifts to the wounded world?

I started an inspirational blog in late 2008 as a personal journal that focused on my photographic art blended with my stories and poetry. That same year saw my artwork exhibited in local and regional exhibitions. Eventually, when I submitted one of my photographs for her artist's gallery, a magazine editor suggested I combine my images with my stories. My "Healing Spirit Art©" fine art photography was now featured in articles that included my stories and poetry. Like a peaceful lake, I was filling up and spilling over.

On a photographic venture in Fairfield County, in October of 2009, I watched a spectacular fall afternoon solar and cloud show over Lake Monticello. I felt touched by the Divine Spirit, in awe of the beauty around me, and at one with peace and love as the sun dropped like a giant orange ball directly behind the Monticello Methodist Church.

Looking over my photographs, I see that the light always leads the eye through my pictures. And so, I keep my faith and trust in the Light, and walk on.

If, as Dr. Emoto said, our words can change a drop of water, just imagine how our acts of kindness influence the lives of strangers. A single thought can influence mass consciousness in a positive and life-changing way. Just for today, let us join together and remember our world as it truly is meant to be.

"It is the true man who leads the mystic life
Whoever is human, whoever dares."
~ Yunus Emre, Sufi mystic (1238-1320)

Mystical South Carolina

Singing Trees

6

Singing Trees of 601: Heaven and Nature

"The most beautiful thing we can experience is the mysterious. It is the source of all true art and science."
~ Albert Einstein (1879-1955)

Once in 2009, on my return journey home from a business trip to Hampton County, I found myself on Highway 601, enjoying the end of the day with my car windows rolled down as I drove through the countryside. Off to the west of me I could feel the Savannah River and the state of Georgia, and off to the east, the Atlantic Ocean and Edisto Beach, a favorite of locals in Hampton County.

The landscape I was driving through, the southwest portion of South Carolina, is still recovering energetically and spiritually from the ravages of war. Native peoples were exterminated or displaced from here. Bloody Revolutionary War battles were fought here. A century later, General Sherman targeted the area after his catastrophic scorched-earth March to the Sea in Georgia. Given the history of this corner of the state, the resilience of Nature and the people who live here are truly amazing. As I recovered from my own struggles, I was becoming more sensitive to the historic trauma of the land.

I was brought up in a Protestant family, attending Methodist churches with my mom and Lutheran churches with my dad, but these days I was exploring spiritual matters from different religions and beliefs. I studied the writings of Catholic mystics such as Saint Hildegard of Bingen, Saint Francis, Saint Bernard of Clairvaux, and Father John O'Donahue. I visited a Hindu temple, an Islamic mosque, and a Buddhist center in my hometown. In one form or another, I always found *music* twining around the holy.

Music has been, and continues to be, an integral part of healing for me. Ancient civilizations knew that music is based on numbers and deeply influences the human heart. I feel myself being made whole when I listen to sound healing through voice, as offered by Tom Kenyon and Jonathan Goldman, or through instruments, as offered by healing harpists Lisa Lynne and Tami Briggs.

That day, as I glided along on Highway 601, all of a sudden the light shifted and the scenery took on a soft, strange glow. Slowing down, I heard a humming sound that grew louder as I approached a grove of trees. As the road dipped and turned, the sound engulfed me and my car and, for an instant, I felt at one with my surroundings, and knew exactly what was producing the humming—the trees.

Did I experience a portal to another dimension that day? I'd encountered a similar awakening to a portal once at the ferry/faery crossing at Blair. Albert Einstein (who once visited a plantation called Mayfair, near Blair) said there are multiple time dimensions that exist concurrently. Could there be an opening here that let the Earth's frequency, the Schumann Resonance, break through to be heard?

There is a saying in the metaphysical community: "When the student is ready, the teacher will appear." Everything is in plain sight.

There is still much healing work to be done, both inside us and outside, particularly in the lands that once were battlefields. So when your pilgrimage carries you to these sites of historical mass violence, please give thanks to the Nature spirits of the place. Bless them and send them your healing prayers and thoughts. And for extra healing and comfort for the land, consider purchasing a small bottle of Violet Flame Transmuting Flower Essences from Green Hope Farm, which has been taken to other battlefields such as Gettysburg and used in healing ceremonies there.

Another form of healing that may be brought to battlefields and other places on our planet in need is sound. Artist and author Jill Mattson has spent decades researching this topic and her music and books are wonderful resources. One of her books is devoted to Sharry Edwards, a modern day trailblazer in the field of sound healing and bioacoustics. Ms. Edwards has heard trees singing, too.

"The earth has music for those who listen."
~ William Shakespeare (1564-1617)

Lilies at Landsford Canal, Catawba River

7

Landsford Canal: The Language of Flowers

"Yes, flowers have tones -- God gave to each
A language of its own,
And bade the simple blossom teach
Where'er its seeds are sown"
Catherine H. Waterman Esling (1812 - 1897)

Floriography, communicating meaning through flowers, has been practiced for thousands of years. The Victorians wrote many books on the language of flowers. Each bloom conveyed a certain meaning. Today, that language is mostly lost on us. We have become sadly oblivious to the rich vocabulary of symbols which appear in almost every aspect of our lives today, flowers among them. A great loss. Centuries ago, artists and their patrons were more aware of these languages. Their "codebooks" still exist, old books detailing their interpretation of symbols—fascinating reading.

All of this came to mind while I was looking through some pictures I took during a trip to the Landsford Canal in Chester County. A fellow photographer and I went to see the world-famous Rocky Shoals spider lilies in full bloom on the Catawba River near the end of May in 2009. Landsford Canal State Park, only an hour's drive from the state capital, is home to the largest population of this floral species on Earth.

When these lilies bloom, emerging from crevices in exposed rocks along the river, it is a spectacle to see. I have looked at some exceptional photographs of the lilies, but no matter how fine the picture, it still pales in comparison with seeing them in person. Children delight in the spidery white blossoms, and adults seeing them feel like children again.

In this beautiful state park, a walk up the shady river path takes you past a tree-lined bluff with a lovely vista. I stopped here on trips home from business meetings just for the walk, the view, and the cool breezes that clear the cobwebs from a dusty mind. The path along the Catawba River is easily navigable on foot or in a wheelchair, so it is a nice outing for all. A wooden dock platform sits on the riverbank and affords a wonderful view of the snow-white blooms. This is a fordable part of the Catawba (hence the "ford" in "Landsford") and you may also see folks in hip-waders walking around in the middle of the river. Local boat rental companies can give you an up-close-and-personal view of the lilies on leisurely downstream floats.

What you are witnessing when the lilies bloom on the Catawba River is a sacred glimpse into the Americas before European settlers arrived. Today this particular flower is only found in three states in the Southern United States: South Carolina, Georgia, and Alabama. There are other rocky rivers where these lilies bloom; however, the Landsford Canal area is the largest community. Like all living beings, the lilies need the right environment to live and prosper. Thanks to the efforts of conservationists such as the Catawba Nation and the late Tommy Wyche of Greenville, the rocky shoals spider lily continues its beautiful legacy.

Just twelve miles away from Landsford Canal State Park, you will find the lands of today's Catawba Indian Nation at Rock Hill, along the western banks of the Catawba River, on the ley lines that flow beside the river. Both Landsford Canal and the Catawba Nation lands, along with Blair and Lake Monticello, are part of the "Olde English District" tourism district of South Carolina.

I have always been drawn to both Landsford and the Catawba Indian Nation. There is an invisible energy that connects the two places along the Catawba River, which originates in the Blue Ridge Mountains in North Carolina and winds its way east and then south into South Carolina. Unlike the northern portion of the Catawba River, the area between Landsford Canal and The Catawba Indian Nation is unspoiled by man-made dams and overdevelopment. South of the Canal is Great Falls and further downstream is a modern-era lake and the Wateree River. The water's meandering path is itself a mystical, harmonious pilgrimage.

The center of Catawba cultural and administrative life is the Longhouse, a circular building with a dodecagon (twelve-sided) roof and a windowed tower obelisk sprouting from the top. The roundness of the building may signify the Medicine Wheel. Or it may embody a flower. For me, the upward-striving design connects Heaven and Earth, a reminder that "as above, so below." A circular space for outdoor ceremonies and meetings lies next to the river. A wonderful museum and gift store feature the world-renowned Catawba pottery. And if you feel like a taking a nice, leisurely stroll, there's a beautiful, wooded walk to the river's edge.

As I increasingly feel the connection of the land to the self, so many questions bubble up from this river. Was the Canal previously part of the Catawba weirs for catching fish? Another name for Catawba is Ye iswa'here, "the People of the River." How does the word "Iswa" or "Issa" (river) relate to the Egyptian goddess of peace and love, Isis' name? Are the Catawba, like the ancient Celtic Druids part of the keepers of the energy grid of Mother Earth?

While completing this book, I had a visit from the spirit of a departed acquaintance, Sue, who had lived in Winnsboro. Sue showed me the interconnectedness of the Catawba and Congaree tribes. The Congaree tribe was devastated by smallpox and other disasters brought by European settlers. Some Congaree melded into other tribes, like the Catawba, until the tribe ceased to exist on its own. Sue showed me that she and I had, in another life, been sisters and members of the Congaree, and we had married into the Catawba tribe.

A historical tidbit: The Catawba are a matriarchal or matrilineal society that once leased part of the 144,000 acres of land, given to them by the King of England, to European settlers. The number 144, or 12 squared, in sacred geometry relates to consciousness and the Divine Feminine.

"In all things in Nature, there is something of the marvelous."
~ Aristotle

Mystical South Carolina

Old Sheldon Church

8

Old Sheldon Church: The Stonehenge of the South

"Here lies the great gift of the Spirit: though we may have lost our way, when we come to that realization, we discover the path once again."
~ Lauren Artress (1945-)

In the early 1970s, my maternal grandfather purchased a small plot of land and built a circular home in the marshlands off St. Helena Island, just outside of Beaufort. I fondly remember many idyllic moments spent in the Spanish-moss-draped Low Country: I witnessed a baptism in a tidal creek there near Frogmore, with the white-robed participants wading into Nature's waters of Love in a way that is seldom seen today. I saddled up and took my first ride on a Marsh Tacky named Mary on a dusty back road on Horse Island, surrounded by a tomato field. Time spent in the Low Country during my childhood holds a special place in my heart. It was during those years that my family and I first discovered Old Sheldon Church, perched on the western edge of the remaining portion of the old Sheldon Plantation, home to the Bull family from Warwickshire, England.

A little over seventeen miles north of Beaufort, near the little Low Country town of Yemassee, the ruins of Prince William Parish Church nestle among ancient live oaks near the old Sheldon plantation. Affectionately known now as "Old Sheldon Church," her gracious columns and arches beckon to all those who embrace her enduring spirit.

It was many years after those early visits with my family that I found myself back at Old Sheldon on an October afternoon in 2009 just before sunset. My job with a sales company was stressful and challenging, and I was searching for peace. I'd been drawn back to Old Sheldon and the quiet, comforting embrace of her sheltering oaks and her resilient spirit. The ruins brought back many happy memories. I entered her hallowed grounds humbly and thanked her for her tranquility and just enjoyed her shelter for a half hour. My spirit revived, I drove home to Columbia. Less than four months later, I had a new job and moved to a new town.

Based on Greek temple design, like ancient sites honoring the goddesses Aphrodite and Isis, Old Sheldon Church lies on an East-West axis, her front doors facing the setting sun. Also in the Greek style, which followed the Egyptian schools of esoteric knowledge, a spring is located just inside her entrance gates. But how does this sacred site in the Deep South connect back to that mystic lineage?

Centuries ago, the Knights Templar returned to Europe from the Holy Land bearing secret knowledge from the Temple of Solomon. Some believe the Masons inherited these mysteries and passed them along to their brethren. Old maps of Prince William Parish and the surrounding Low Country show a Masonic meeting place near the Sheldon Plantation and the site of the Old Sheldon Church ruins.

Like a great phoenix, Old Sheldon Church has risen regally from her ashes twice. Burned by the British during the Revolutionary War and destroyed again during the Civil War, the outline of her gracious figure still stands. Hundreds make a pilgrimage to her ruins for an annual prayer service on the second Sunday after Easter. Countless others have been happily wedded here.

Like a Stonehenge of the South, the ruins' sacred knowledge and sacred geometry play a role, along with the Nature spirits of this place, in guiding pilgrims on our path, reorienting us when we have lost our direction.

A portion of the old Sheldon Plantation has recently been sold and you can view photographs of it on the internet. Now part of the ACE Basin, named for the preserved lands between the Ashepoo, Combahee, and Edisto rivers, this sacred site continues to hold the mystery and grace of the landscape around it.

"One place understood helps us understand all places better"
~ Eudora Welty (1909-2001)

The Path of the Unknown Souls

Across the sea of mystic dreams,
Three ships came in the night,
and moored near marshlands
out of sight.

This cargo, precious, filled
with darkness and light,
and secrets kept from ages past,
do now, in the present unfold.

For I have seen
the mystery,
and walked the path
of the unknown souls.

Mom Walking the Labyrinth

9

Lutheran Theological Southern Seminary: Walking the Labyrinth

"Truly, the greatest gift you have to give is that of your own self-transformation."
~*Lao Tzu (601 BCE-?)*

Life kept battering me. I continued my hectic travels with work. I was subjected to stalking by my landlord's stepson and harassed by my employer. Upon returning home from one long drive for a business trip in the summer of 2009, my kneecap twisted suddenly out of its socket and I fell on the floor in agony. This was a wake-up call, but I kept on pushing myself, working and driving.

A mention of labyrinths in one of my many inspirational books, followed by a search on the internet, led me to the labyrinth at the Lutheran Theological Southern Seminary in Columbia. The Lutheran Theological Southern Seminary is now part of the Lenoir-

Rhyne University in Hickory, North Carolina, so this labyrinth had something in common with other sacred sites in this book—the Catawba River runs through Hickory on the way to South Carolina, the Catawba Indian Nation, and the Landsford Canal.

This particular example was a fortunate choice to begin my study of labyrinths. One of fifty-two labyrinths in South Carolina listed on the World Wide Labyrinth Locator, its "dromenon" design is based on the medieval labyrinth at Chartres Cathedral in France.

Chartres Cathedral was built by an unknown architect with the help of the surrounding community. Men and women, rich and poor, all shared in the building of this great cathedral. It is believed by many that Chartres is a monument to the oneness of us all, humanity, nature, and God. It became a pilgrimage site for followers of Mother Mary, a symbol of the Divine Feminine Presence. Once they arrived at Chartres, pilgrims' prayers did not have to go through a priest or other church representative in order to reach Heaven. By praying to Mother Mary, the pilgrims believed their prayers were taken directly to God.

The Divine Feminine Presence is part of the sacred union of the Father/Mother aspects of the Divine Spirit, or God. For millennia, the Divine Feminine has been suppressed by patriarchal societies. In the past century, we have witnessed a great resurgence of rights and respect for the Feminine in many countries, but this ever-growing movement still meets with resistance in many parts of the globe.

On a sunny Thanksgiving Day in 2009, my mother and I walked the labyrinth at the Lutheran Theological Southern Seminary together for the first and only time. Less than a year later, I received a phone call at work that Mom, my best friend, had passed away suddenly and unexpectedly in her home.

My mother and I were very close, and it took me a long time to process my grief. As part of my healing process, I decided to take the day off on the first anniversary of her passing, and spend time at a beautiful place surrounded by nature, communing with her spirit. This became an annual tradition, along with remembering her birthday and celebrating Mother's Day.

Walking the labyrinth has been part of my pilgrimage of healing. Unknown to me at the time of my first walk on this labyrinth, it was an initiation into reconnecting my soul with the Divine Feminine Presence. I only knew then that this exercise brought me peace in a challenging time in my life. Walking the concentric circles of the labyrinth and finding my way to the Center reminds me to go within to find God. Stepping off the treadmill of constant work and worries, I let go and let God.

Shortly prior to the first anniversary of Mom's passing, one of my clients stopped by my office. She told me that her mother had passed away a few years before—she understood what I was experiencing. Then she shared an extraordinary insight. She said after her mother passed, she was experiencing very painful grief. In the midst of her sobbing and tears she cried out, "Who is going to love me now that you are gone?" And in the stillness she heard a gentle and reassuring reply. "You will."

As I made my way through the labyrinth of grief and on to the remaining sites discussed in this book, I walked through great feelings of grief and loss. In mourning deeply, I learned a lot about myself.

When we allow ourselves to fully experience our emotions, we benefit in profound ways. Emotions are not who we are, they are simply a way our physical bodies respond to life. We are not their prisoner or their victims. We, in collaboration with our emotions, create our own realities. This knowledge in itself is empowering.

Walking the labyrinth helps synchronize body and mind, conscious and unconscious, masculine and feminine, right- and left-hemisphere. In the truest pilgrim fashion, it helps us become whole.

"All shall be well"
~ Julian of Norwich (1342-1416)

Mystical South Carolina

Ricefields at Middleton Place

10

Middleton Place: The Labyrinth in the Rice Fields

""Lord, make me an instrument of thy peace.
Where there is hatred, let me sow love..."
~ St. Francis of Assisi (1181/82-1226)

December has always brought many blessings to me. Traveling through my home state opens my eyes to the beauty of this season. Solstice, Yule, Christmas, Kwanzaa, Hanukkah, and the New Year bring their celebrations. Spiced eggnog and my mom's colorful, delicious cookies added good cheer and happiness to the month of holidays. Delivering gifts to friends on Boxing Day, the English holiday on the day after Christmas, is always a delight. Truly a season of peace on Earth, goodwill toward all.

During one December trip in the Low Country in late 2009, I stopped to have lunch at the Woodlands Mansion in Summerville.

Before my journey, I had researched labyrinths in this part of the state and decided to visit one at nearby Middleton Place, a plantation just twenty minutes away from Woodlands.

Mother Earth was once again changing her wardrobe. The labyrinth at Middleton turned out to be mowed into the grass at the entrance to the rice fields a short walk from the Inn at Middleton Place. The rice fields are lovely in December. Wildlife abounds. As I walked the labyrinth, and the rice fields, Middleton Place gifted me with muted photographs of winter spiced with the colors of nutmeg, cinnamon, cloves, and a little ginger. The time and foresight of the English-style landscape design creates an elegant terrain here, carved from land that was once wilderness. It is truly an artist's and writer's delight, a place of contemplation and creativity.

The natural beauty of this place once held the not-so-beautiful story of slavery. In the 1970s, descendants of those slaveholders transferred ownership of the plantation to the Middleton Place Foundation, which maintains the 6,000 acre site and keeps it open to the public. A new and kinder story is being written through the efforts of a 20th century Middleton descendant, Charles Duell.

Arthur Middleton was one of the signers of the Declaration of Independence. At that time in history, it was a daring document to put your name on. By signing it, Arthur risked his own life, his family's lives, and his home. "All men are created equal," it said, "and endowed by their creator with certain inalienable rights." Those grand ideals, however, did not apply to women, slaves, and Native Americans—only to white men of European descent. That was the level of consciousness of the time.

But times have changed at Middleton Place. The history of the slaves that toiled here (including births, deaths, and marriages) is honored as a precious legacy and the Foundation makes this history available for those researching genealogy. So, in a strange twist of fate, the old Middleton plantation is rescuing Black history from the shadows, providing information to African-Americans about their roots as it continues to explore and bring to light the stories of all the inhabitants of this place.

The Ashley River runs through and by Middleton Place and flows down to Charleston and the Atlantic Ocean, passing by other former plantations. A museum is being built on the steps of the Gadsden Wharf in Charleston, where slaves from Africa first set foot on American soil. The first CEO and president of this International African American Museum is a descendant of Africans kidnapped from a small village in Sierra Leone, a country from which tens of thousands of people were transported to Charleston to be enslaved. His ancestors arrived at Gadsden Wharf.

If we believe that everything is in Divine Order, then can we imagine that America's murderous treatment of its Native peoples and enslavement of kidnapped Africans is somehow part of what is bringing our nation into greater consciousness now? Looking at and acknowledging all aspects of ourselves, both Shadows and Light, can we bring about true transformation, both personal and national?

There is a great opportunity in Middleton Place to create prayers for reconciliation and forgiveness. In ancient Egypt, on the continent from which the African slaves were kidnapped, there was a school of knowledge that taught if one could swim the Nile

River without being attacked and eaten by crocodiles, then one had mastered one's thoughts. For thoughts are our own creations, and mastering our fears brings us in harmony with love. We attract what our thoughts, both conscious and subconscious, project. Perfect love casts out fear. What the heart sows, grows, and these old rice fields can be sown afresh with seeds of healing. You can help with this work while walking the labyrinth and meditating on the kindness that can be. Another opportunity to grow the nurturing Divine Feminine Presence in our world.

A rice field is a powerful place to sow seeds of a new consciousness. Imagine hundreds of people of all races, holding hands and encircling these fields once worked by slaves. Imagine them singing songs of peace and love in harmony and unity. Imagine them releasing old hurts and beliefs programmed since birth. Imagine them sitting down together to share a delicious meal amongst the gifts of God's beautiful landscape. Imagine them harvesting a new world. Imagine this land healing.

Humanity has inflicted wounds on each other that have lasted for generations. May these rice/race fields be the site of great healing for all, and may the rivers flow forgiveness and peace throughout the land and back across the ocean.

"*The nutmeg has a great warmth in its powers. And if a man eats a nutmeg, it opens his heart and gives him a good, clear mind.*

Take nutmeg and in the same weight cinnamon and some cloves, and pulverize all. Make tartlets with this powder, with flour and little water, and eat them often.

It will damp the bitterness of the heart and clean the dull senses, and it makes your spirit happy and reduces all bad humors in you and will give your blood a good humor and makes you strong."

~ Hildegard von Bingen, Christian mystic (1098-1179)

Archway

11

Pearl Fryar's Topiary Garden: Love, Peace and Goodwill

"A good story is like a compass, it points to something true and invites us to orient our own direction according to it and perhaps to live a little better."
~ Dr. Rachel Naomi Remen (1938-)

Near the heart of South Carolina, just a mile from Interstate 20, there is a living sculpture garden created by Mr. Pearl Fryar. The topiary that lives with Pearl and his family is extraordinary. It challenges the minds of horticulture experts—these plants aren't supposed to be able to look like they do.

I have visited Pearl's garden of surreal trees and shrubs several times. My first visit was on October 14, 2011, the first anniversary of my mother's passing. Mom and I had watched the documentary "A Man Named Pearl" on our local PBS station several months before she died; neither of us had heard of his garden before then. We decided to go and visit. Sadly, Mom passed away before we could see Pearl's garden together.

So on a sunny autumn day, I drove alone from my home in Camden to Bishopville. The Lynches River, just east of Mr. Pearl's now world-famous topiary garden and Highway 15, flows south towards the Atlantic Ocean. Cotton once grew in abundance here, worked by enslaved people. In fact, Mr. Pearl's transformed land is part of an old crop field. I stopped for lunch at the local Waffle House adorned with Pearl's signature-style topiary outside the front door and a "Mr. Pearl Special" on the menu, a good start to a memorable afternoon.

The mission of the Pearl Fryar Topiary Garden is to "support and preserve the artistic and horticultural legacy of Pearl Fryar, to encourage public appreciation of the garden, and to provide opportunities for artistic and educational enrichment and enjoyment." I will always remember my first impression of this amazing playground of the imagination. Located on a short, quiet side-street off the main road entering Bishopville, the garden sits on the left side of the road. A bank of pine trees lends shade and depth at the back of the property. There are two distinct areas: Pearl's brick ranch-house stands on the right side of the property and an archway leads visitors to the left.

When I stepped through this archway into Pearl's wonderland for the first time, I was met by gigantic letters that could be read from space, cut into the grass and planted with red begonias, spelling out the words "Love, Peace and Goodwill." I felt like I had come home. Tears filled my eyes. My heart began to heal from grief. Your spirit stirs and wakes when you step into this sacred space created by the collaboration of a humble man of God and the plants that he communes with each day.

Born outside Clinton, North Carolina, in 1939, Pearl settled his family on an old cornfield in Bishopville in the late 1970s. He built a home and decided to design a garden so he could compete for his town's Yard of the Month award. Unfortunately, his land fell just outside the city limits, so he was not eligible.

Undeterred, Pearl kept looking for something unique for his new garden. He found it a short drive away in Camden. A local plant nursery had some topiary for sale and Pearl asked how the plant-sculptures were created. So the owner gave Pearl a three-minute class and the rest is history. From that brief lesson, Pearl went back home and began to shape topiary in every spare moment in his time off from work at the local aluminum can factory—an amazing feat considering he did not even know the meaning of the word until that lesson.

Webster's dictionary defines topiary as "the practice or art of training, cutting, and trimming trees or shrubs into odd or ornamental shapes." It's an art that takes time, patience, commitment, and creativity. Some of the living statues in Pearl's garden have been twenty years and longer in the making. Pearl has taken this art form to new levels and from its humble beginnings his garden is now known world-wide, attracting more than 10,000 visitors annually.

Always the consummate host, Pearl makes all of his guests feel welcomed and special. As able to communicate with people as with plants, he is a true ambassador for his craft. He had no guild to teach him his art, and yet he still became a master.

From the first time I met Mr. Pearl, I knew that he was a very special soul with an incredible mission here on Earth. He is the kind of person who has a unique gift of connecting with people and plants. He speaks to our hearts, and energetically holds the space between us, allowing each person to feel their own Divinity. He sees our True Self, our soul. It is a special blessing to be in his presence.

In April 2015, Mr. Pearl was part of my onstage production *Seasons of the South—the Original Home-Grown Musical and Storytelling Show*, in Camden. He read one of my poems, "Faith, Hope, and Taking Chances," and it was magical to hear my thoughts read to an audience by a person I so admire. Like Leonardo da Vinci, Pearl is a master artist and his creations and his legacy are international and lasting.

While you are in Bishopville, you can also visit the South Carolina Cotton Museum and get someone to tell you the story of the Lizard Man of Scape Ore Swamp. Scape Ore Swamp is fed by artesian springs, so even if you miss seeing the Lizard Man you can go home with some artesian spring water if you come prepared with a jug or two.

"Proudest moment in your life is if you feel you've influenced somebody positively."
~ Pearl Fryar (1940-)

Faith, Hope, and Taking Chances

Some men search for it all their lives.
Some look a long time, some look a short time.
Some choose not to look for it at all
and thus lose hope and faith in life.

All of us want it, yet some will not take the chance to find it.
For them, the risk means pain
and that is a price they will not pay.

It finds all that take the chance to look for it.
Once found, a wise man pays the price to keep it.
For the true kind is the best and the one worth all the risk.

Once found, it will bring pure joy, add hope, chase away all doubts and fears, and bring light to the dark.

And it does not ask for a thing.

*The warmth it gives can be spread—
a gift to all that will take it, and share it.
It can bond all men as one, if they let it.
It has the strength to end all wars,
stop plagues and droughts.*

*What a shame that all the world
does not know it, for it will
share with young and old, rich and poor, black and white.
The risk is so small, and the gain is so great.
Yet some are still blind to its ways.*

*What a day it will be—
When the whole world finds love.*

White Mountain Laurel Flowers

12

Kalmia Gardens: The Divine Feminine Presence

"Here is my secret. It's quite simple. One sees clearly only with the heart. Anything essential is invisible to the eyes."
~ The Little Prince,
by Antoine de Saint-Exupery (1900-1944)

Have you ever spent time in a garden, and found yourself weeping softly with joy from merely being in the presence of the flowers?

Children understand this. Very few grown-ups do.

About twenty minutes northeast of Bishopville on the South Carolina Cotton Trail, you can let your heart open in Hartsville's thirty-acre botanical heaven, Kalmia Gardens. The lush green surroundings envelope visitors with a glow from Nature's own heartland. Green, the color of the heart chakra, permeates the slow-winding Black Creek's tannin-tinted water as it reflects back the canopy's green hues as if a fairy forest lay below its surface. Paths wind up and down along the sixty-foot drop from the historic Hart family home to the banks of Black Creek, the gateway to the surrounding cypress-kneed swampland.

Spending an afternoon in the gardens at Kalmia has a deeply calming effect. The afternoon sun peeks through fluffy white clouds and the canopy of pines, oaks, and hollies and gives the land a special glow. In the springtime when the mountain laurel are blooming, their faceted pink blooms render an especially happy aura. Taking in their gift is very therapeutic. If you look closely, you can count the ten points in the center of the flowers. Meditatively meandering along the pathways strewn with flower petals, the quiet stillness permeates and soothes your heart and soul. A person loses track of time easily here. In Jorge Luis Borges's words, "To gaze at a river made of time and water and remember Time is another river."

The Divine Feminine Presence fills this place, channeled by the founder and architect of the gardens, Mrs. David Robert Coker—"Miss May," as she is affectionately remembered by the locals. Miss May shared a love of camellias and azaleas with Arthur Middleton's progeny at Middleton Place. Folks thought she was a tad eccentric back in 1932 when she started laying trails, digging ponds, and planting the azaleas, wisterias, tea olives, and camelias that would transform thirty acres of rugged bluff wilderness into today's Kalmia Gardens. So don't worry if you feel a bit of divine madness when you experience the splendors of Kalmia; eighty-plus years on, the only ones laughing now are us kids enjoying time with the flowers and the fairies, on the pathway to joy.

The Coker family lends their name to the local college as well, and their Sonoco Products Company has deep roots in cotton culture, starting with the production of cones for cotton spinning. Sonoco is South Carolina's largest corporation (in terms of sales) and has garnered respect and awards for its corporate responsibility and sustainability practices.

Musically, Hartsville is famous for Renofest, a world-class bluegrass festival which for twenty years honored banjo legend Don Reno.

Water, flowers, and the harmony of music: all elements of the sacred and a great combination for lifting the spirits of the pilgrim.

"Love and compassion are necessities, not luxuries. Without them humanity cannot survive."
~ The Fourteenth Dalai Lama (1935-)

Awareness

Being aware of our awareness,
Being conscious and igniting
Recognition of our thoughts.

Allowing our inner self
To kindle the flame of the
Light of Creation.

Giving ourselves the peaceful time
And allowing our spirit to soak
In the wonder and joy of our
Life, and walking forward
With the Grace of God,
And strength and ease.

And accepting the wisdom of
Honoring our souls.

This is our gift, our legacy
For generations to come.

Knowing who we really are
And living our life mission
Joyfully and abundantly.

I am a Lightworker
And Truth is my guide.
The light of peace is my
Torch that illuminates
My footpath and leads
My way, even when all seems
Dark and it feels like
The road is lost.

For to wander is to travel
Down the lane of eternity,
And find one's self again,
Forever safe and loved
And Blessed.

For Love is the answer,
That begins with our own self.
Always and forever.
Amen.

Mystical South Carolina

Bridge to Unknowing

Postscript

"Faith, hope, and love. But the greatest of these is Love."
~ I Corinthians 13:13

Many moons have passed since I jotted down my first notes on this project, and now I write this postscript from my home in the Blue Ridge Mountains of Western North Carolina. As a child, my family and I visited both these mountains and the Low Country around Beaufort and Charleston at the end of our summers, so I developed a great fondness for this part of the world. I can't imagine a better place to put the finishing touches on this book.

As this book-pilgrimage was drawing to an end, early one morning a message from the Light appeared outside my window. Through the leaves of the trees here in the Nantahala Forest, the rising sun sent dots of lights coding the letters "M," "X," and "A": "M" for "Mu," Hawaiian for water, "X" for chi or life force, and "A" for "Alpha" or beginning. Water is the source of all life.

For most of my life I have lived near water. Now I am blessed to live in a National Forest with a spring pond, a creek, a waterfall. I go to sleep with a chorus of crickets and frogs singing lullabies in my ear. Owls hoot. Fireflies dance in the summer, kindling my inner child. My soul settles, soothed, every evening. My spirit is renewed every morning. From the Blue Ridge Mountains come the beginnings, the headwaters of rivers of my birth state, flowing with love to the Atlantic Ocean and beyond.

Rivers. Flow. How did the twelve sacred sites in the book connect to each other? As I wrapped up the manuscript, I felt a great hunger to be able to see all twelve locations on a map, to grasp the Big Picture. I wanted to see how ley lines of energy-flow might relate to the flow of my pilgrimages, so I sought advice. When I found the website of Peter Champoux, author of *Gaia Matrix*, I knew that I had found the right ally. I contacted him and asked for his help.

Several days later I received Peter's reply. When I opened his email and saw the map he had created for me and read his explanatory text, I wept with joy for ten minutes. His remarks give an extraordinary insight into these twelve sites. I had never imagined that they were all linked in such a profound way.

Who could have guessed that these twelve points on the map would form circular rings of energetic love, just waiting to be activated by humans? Like an invisible network of the planet's veins and arteries radiating from the heart of South Carolina, our Mother Earth waits for us to circulate her Flow. As part of the Divine Plan, humanity is meant to live in partnership with Mother Earth. And by simply sending our heartfelt prayers toward the Congaree Swamp, and out through these concentric circles, we can help to heal the world.

What started out as a travel memoir has blossomed to encompass much more. My intention, as I launch this book out into the world, is that the consciousness of all who read it will expand like a beating heart and pump their own prayers for healing out through this incredible network. May we create a river of healing, starting with ourselves.

"An empty lantern provides no light.
Self-care is the fuel that allows your light to shine brightly."
~ Author unknown

What was once unseen and unimagined is now brought to Light. It is said Love is the greatest healer of all and can cast out all fear. Then I cast my prayers for the Light, for Mother Earth, and for all who dwell on this beautiful planet. And I pray that you, dear reader, will join your prayers with mine, percolating out through the Congaree Rings.

There is a sense of urgency as I get these pages ready for printing. Mother Earth has been waiting for our awakening for a long time. She says the time is now and *each* of our gifts is sorely needed to help all beings and the planet herself. For centuries, some of those who have understood how the planetary grid of energy flow works have been using it to create chaos and harm. It is now time for lightworkers to claim our power and send Love and healing to these Congaree Rings. Time to actively cocreate Heaven on Earth, our birthright.

Our Native ancestors and relatives today have known, understood, and practiced their love of Mother Earth for as long as they have walked on this planet. By joining our prayers to theirs, we can help to heal a lot of wounds. I am thankful for all our Native brothers and sisters who have held this vigil for Mother Earth for so long. May we all now be united and grow in strength for this cause.

It is time for the Great Healing. It is time for us to reclaim our power. A gift in plain sight has been given to us. We asked for it long ago and now it is time to receive our gift with thanksgiving.

Let us accept our invitation to send love to the Congaree Rings today.

My pilgrimage continues with gladness and joy, surrounded by new friends and united with old friends here on Earth and those passed on.

May your path be filled with love and light, happiness and joy, prosperity and abundance, thanksgiving and gratitude, kindness and compassion. May you be blessed and highly favored in all ways.

Teri Leigh Teed
Healing Spirit Art©
www.terileighteed.com

When you need help, call upon an artist. Throughout the ages, artists have helped to bring awareness to everything from social inequalities to treatments of illnesses to the welfare of children and animals. Raising consciousness is the great gift of the artist to our world, and it begins with the artist's own transformation.

Mystical South Carolina

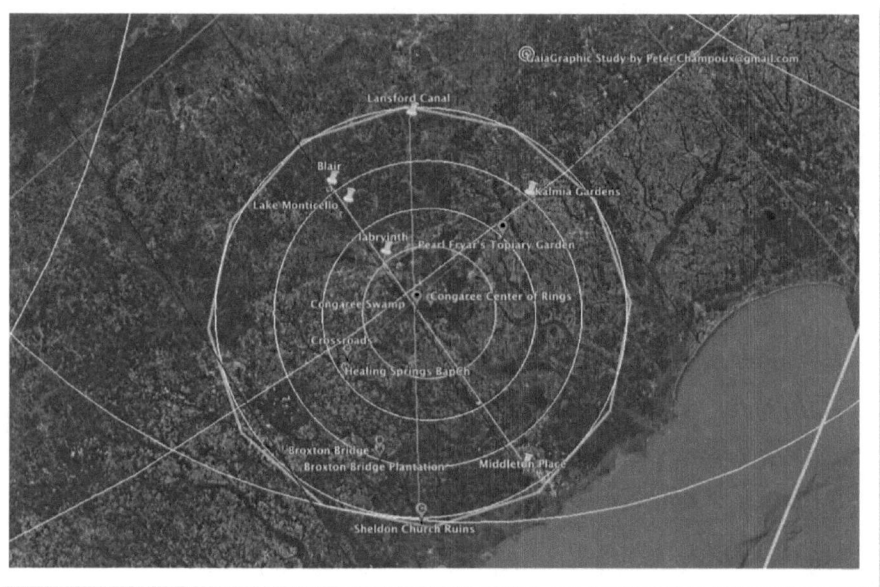

Map of the Twelve Sacred Sites
© *GaiaGraphic Study by Peter Champoux*

The Congaree Rings

What follows is the letter Peter Champoux sent me explaining the energetic relationship of the twelve sites I've introduced you to in this book:

In the accompanying maps and Google Earth .kmz files you will find that your 12 sites cohere into angles that co-align into a 12 sided form or dodecagon -12 sites, 12 sides. This was accomplished with the simple alignments made by the 12 sites; one alignment orienting in a roughly North/ South direction. The common center of these alignments is the Congaree Swamp National Park. Another series orients North-North West to the hydrological center of North America at Lake Itasca, the headwater of the Mississippi River. More on that later. Other site alignment series supported the dodecagon form adding spokes to a wheel.

The N/S Congaree you will note creates a diameter suggestive of a circle, a circle that encompasses most of South Carolina and its river systems. The remaining sites co-generate other regularly spaced rings around 17 miles apart. These rings have a center in the Congaree Swamp but closer to the great confluence at the heart of South Carolina.

These rings and dodecagon are framed by the river leys of Savannah and Great Pee Dee rivers. Indeed the entire works have river leys coursing throughout like radiant stream beaming out from the Moon sized ring centered on Lake Itasca. The 'Congaree Rings' sites on the southern arc of the Pilot Mountain Earth Ring like a gear in the works of the Earth-Motor. Actually these rings appear to function like a cell's Integral Membrane Proteins (IMPs); receiving and transmitting information for planetary health. The array of 12 sites focusing on the vibrating heart of South Carolina would in effect transmit intentioned healing energies into its waters and transmit this coherent love to bio and litho spheres. As water is in motion, in vortex and wave, its motion and emotion as gifted by spirit would set the Pilot Ring in its static spin, cleansing the heart of Dixie, and support the vortexing fields of North America's bubbling rings; whose greatest wheel arc up Central America, California, and around to the Arctic Circle and along the Mid Atlantic Rift, forming a planet balancing yin/yang field half water half land. As an Earth Cell human consciousness is integral to its governing biosphere membrane. Having the moon ring edge of Lake Itasca wheel make Congaree one of the stone of this continental level Medicine Wheel. Congaree, covering the southern quadrant of the Pilot Wheel, soothes the Parris Island USMC toxic masculinity with the waters of the Divine Feminine, working more harmoniously with the Pilot Wheels north pole of Krishna consciousness and spiritual warriorship at Krishna Temple in Moundsville, WV.

Other features of note are the Lei Lines that frame Congaree on three sides: Serpent Mound Lei to the northeast, Broadway Lei (coursing along Broadway in NYC) to the southeast and the Acadian Lei to the northwest whose alignment coheres the east coast cities with the war fields of Europe, the Ottomans, and the Middle East. By spiritually healing the waters to the Congaree they heal the Pilot and the Pilot heals the memories carried as frequency along these great lei alignments and replaces them with the frequency Teri infused into South Carolina's rivers in her Earth-healing work.

There are of course endless earth energies that could be mapped but in the end it would be solid text and line everywhere on the map. Every river has leys coursing along either bank. In total the Congaree Ring is a vortex of vortices connecting South Carolina's rivers in pulsing rings radiating the rivers into the oceans informing those waters that they too are loved and are healed.

Keep up the good work!! Peter

"I shall be love, thus I shall be everything, and thus my dream will be realized."
~ St. Therese of Lisieux, "The Little Flower" (1873-1897)

The Twelve Sacred Sites

"We have it in our power to begin the world over again."
~ Thomas Paine (1737-1809)

To help you create your own mystic journeys, here is a list of the locations of the twelve sacred sites I've discussed in this book:

1. Healing Springs, SC 29817 - 3 miles north of Blackville, SC, on Highway 3, turn right on Healing Springs Rd, behind Healing Springs Baptist Church.

2. Highway 3 (near crossroads) - north of Healing Springs, just north of Springfield Flea Market, 9113 Neeses Highway, Springfield, SC 29146.

3. Congaree National Park - approximately 20 miles south of Columbia, SC. 100 National Park Rd, Hopkins, SC 29061.

4. Blair, SC - midway between Winnsboro, SC, and Newberry, SC, on the Broad River, Highway 34 - 18 miles east of Newberry, SC, and approximately 18 miles west of Winnsboro, SC.

5. Lake Monticello - reservoir next to the Broad River and south of Blair, SC. 75 Baltic Cir, Jenkinsville, SC 29065 (on Highway 215).

6. Highway 601 - between Highway 278 and Highway 641, north of Hampton SC (before Broxton Bridge Civil War battlefield on Highway 641).

7. Landsford Canal—State Park near the Catawba Reservation. 2051 Park Dr, Catawba, SC 29704.

8. Old Sheldon Church - on the Bull family's Sheldon Plantation, approximately 17 miles north of Beaufort, SC. Old Sheldon Church Rd, Yemassee, SC 29945.

9. Lutheran Theological Southern Seminary – Chartres-style labyrinth, 4201 N Main St, Columbia, SC 29203.

10. Middleton Place - rice fields and labyrinth in grass, about 15 miles northwest of Charleston. 4300 Ashley River Rd, Charleston, SC 29414.

11. Pearl Fryar's Topiary Garden - 145 Broad Acres Rd, Bishopville, SC 29010.

12. Kalmia Gardens - 1624 W Carolina Ave, Hartsville, SC 29550.

"Once you fully realize the situation then you will know what to do. And then spread that information to others."
~ Greta Thunberg (2003-)

Acknowledgments

"How far that little candle throws his beams!
So shines a good deed in a weary world."
~ The Merchant of Venice,
by William Shakespeare (1564-1616)

For seven years I followed an intuitively led path to sacred sites throughout my home state. Another seven years passed before I completed and published this book. There are so many who have helped me during this pilgrimage and I am most thankful.

To my mom, who always encouraged me to write and was herself a most excellent role model. I love you and you are always in my heart.

For all my friends and companions who traveled with me during some of my visits to the sacred sites on this pilgrimage: Bob Medlock, Jim Murphy, Susan Grey, Keith and Charmaine Cross.

To my dear friends who have provided unwavering assistance and support:

To Joan Meeting, my childhood friend who has always been there to lend a kind hand and with whom I share many happy memories.

To Scott Johnson, a special thank you because anyone who helps you move is a saint in my book.

To Dorothy Johnson, who has been my friend for so long, and has supported me like a sister.

My family at Cathedral of Praise in Camden: Bishop Thomas C. Bell, Pamela Jones, Linda Briggs, and all of my brothers and sisters. Thank you for allowing me to be part of your energy of love and joy, and great music.

To Phyllis David, Linda Higgins, Julia Halford, Kay Roberson, Phyllis Morris Wainscott, in Camden, much love for all your kindness. And to Ann Myers, dear friend rest in peace.

Mystical South Carolina

To Nancy Heil and dear departed Bill, and Kenny and Lisa, my deep thanks for treating me like family.

To my dear friends in Sylva, North Carolina: Marsha Crites, Joan and Ernie Sipler, and Lena and Oval Richie. Blessings for all your help and encouragement.

To Nadia Mostafa, my beautiful friend and yoga teacher. Thank you for the light you continuously bring to our world, and for your grace.

To Lee Rumble, for your kindness and listening and for bringing much light to this world. Rest in peace, dear friend.

To the SCIway.net and South Carolina Picture Project team, for allowing me to be part of your sites and for displaying my photographs and stories about the special places in my home state.

To the Olde English District team, Jayne Scarborough and Strauss Shiple, for giving me the opportunity to serve on your Board and for supporting me in my artistic ventures.

To Duane Parrish and the team at the South Carolina Parks, Recreation, and Tourism Department, many thanks for your time and support.

To Shaila Abdullah, my wonderful book and website designer, author of *Saffron Dreams* and *Beyond the Cayenne Wall*. Thank you for your guidance and expertise.

To Donna Glee Williams, author of *Dreamers and The Braided Path*, for her editing prowess and creative insights.

To Emile DeFelice, Erin Curtis, Heather Curtis and the team at Soda City and the Gervais Street Bridge Dinner, for helping me to launch my first book in style.

To Lynn McTaggert, for helping me to learn about and experience the power of intention. And to my dear sisters of my Intention Circle in North Carolina, blessings to you always.

To Sanjay Nimar, for your compassion, acceptance, and remembrance. Thank you for helping me remember my wholeness and joy.

To Renee Phillips, Founder and Director of Manhattan Arts International and Healing Power of ART & ARTISTS, thank you for your kind words and encouragement.

Resources

"In the course of history, there comes a time when humanity is called to shift to a new level of consciousness, to reach a higher moral ground. A time when we have to shed our fear and give hope to each other. That time is now."
~ Wangari Maathai (1940 -2011)

Foreword

Rumi. https://en.wikipedia.org/wiki/Rumi

Chapter 1 - Healing Springs

South Carolina Picture Project, a part of the SCIway.net information sites. A marvelous font of information. Please consider being a contributor and sending your own photographs and stories. https://www.scpictureproject.org/barnwell-county/healing-springs.html

Chapter 2 - Cathedral of Highway 3

Information on Highway 3. https://en.wikipedia.org/wiki/South_Carolina_Highway_3

Chapter 3 - Congaree Swamp

Congaree National Park. https://www.nps.gov/cong/index.htm

Ken Carey, *Return of the Bird Tribes*. https://www.harpercollins.com/9780062116567/return-of-the-bird-tribes/

TED Talk by Ted Stangler, Congaree Riverkeeper - Rivers Belong to All of Us. https://www.youtube.com/watch?v=ltdqeqqsVko

TED Talk by Nixiwaka Yawanawa – We Are All Connected with Nature. https://www.youtube.com/watch?v=xk0-yebNA_o

Chapter 4 - Blair

SC Picture Project. https://www.scpictureproject.org/fairfield-county/blair-general-store.html

Olde English District. https://www.oldeenglishdistrict.com/

Susan Grey, distance healer. https://www.distancehealer.net/

Chapter 5 - Lake Monticello

SC Picture Project. https://www.scpictureproject.org/fairfield-county/lake-monticello.html

SC Great Outdoors. https://scgreatoutdoors.com/park-lakemonticello.html

SC Department of Natural Resources. http://www.dnr.sc.gov/lakes/monticello/description.html

Chapter 6 - The Singing Trees of 601

Jill Mattson. https://www.jillswingsoflight.com/

Sharry Edwards—BioAcoustics. https://soundhealthoptions.com/

"You Can Talk to Plants. Maybe You Should Listen" by JoAnna Klein. https://www.nytimes.com/2019/06/11/science/plant-sounds-brooklyn-botanic-garden.html

"Flowers can hear buzzing bees, and it makes their nectar sweeter" by Michelle Z. Donahue. https://www.nationalgeographic.com/science/2019/01/flowers-can-hear-bees-and-make-their-nectar-sweeter/

The Harmonagon Project—"The Geometry of Music." https://www.youtube.com/watch?v=ZWzwb4BumIk

Jonathan Goldman. https://www.healingsounds.com/

Tom Kenyon. https://tomkenyon.com/

Green Hope Farm Flower Essences. https://www.greenhopeessences.com/

Chapter 7 - Landsford Canal

SC PRT. https://southcarolinaparks.com/landsford-canal

SC Picture Project. https://www.scpictureproject.org/chester-county/landsford-canal-state-park.html

SC Department of Archives and History—Landsford Canal

Per this site information, "The tract, including an aboriginal ford, was granted to Thomas Land in 1754, thus the derivation of its name." Before Thomas Land owned the tract, it was part of the Catawba Nation. http://www.nationalregister.sc.gov/chester/S10817712001/index.htm

Catawba Indian Nation. http://catawbaindian.net/

Catawba Nation v. South Carolina – history of the land ownership of the Catawba Nation. narf.org/nill/documents/nlr/nlr9-4.pdf

Thomas J. Blumer Collection on the Catawba Nation. http://scmemory.org/collection/t-j-blumer-collection-of-the-catawba-indian/

Catawba River. https://en.wikipedia.org/wiki/Catawba_River

History of the Catawba River. https://catawba.naturalresources.anthro-seminars.net/history-of-catawba-river/

Catawba River Keeper. https://www.catawbariverkeeper.org/2017/03/28/top-10-great-places-visit-catawba-basin/

Catawba—Wateree River Basin Map Explorer. http://catawba.maps.arcgis.com/apps/webappviewer/index.html?id=86a805d54d5546d2b99a73d60b16a19d

http://www.naturalandtrust.org/spider-lily-preserve

Chapter 8 - Old Sheldon Church

SC Picture Project. https://www.scpictureproject.org/beaufort-county/old-sheldon-church.html/

Looking at Peter Champoux's map of the twelve sacred sites, I pondered the connection shown by the line between Old Sheldon Church ruins and Landsford Canal and the Catawba Nation lands. A search through historical records brought this to light.

William Bull (1683-1755) commissioned "Old Sheldon" church, or chapel of ease, because it was constructed close to the homes of those who found it easier to travel there instead of the parish church. He died prior to the completion of the church and is buried inside near the pulpit. http://www.scencyclopedia.org/sce/entries/bull-william/

William Bull II (September 24, 1710 - July 4, 1791)—His sister was married to Henry Middleton of Middleton Plantation. Due to his political beliefs, Bull left South Carolina after the Revolution and died in London. "Just like his father and grandfather, William II negotiated with the Native Americans including a treaty with the Catawba Indians of South Carolina and Iroquiois Confederacy as well as a peace treaty that ended the Cherokee War of 1763 that was signed at Ashley Hall Plantation. He also served as acting governor of South Carolina five separate times between 1760 and 1775." https://south-carolina-plantations.com/charleston/ashley-hall.html

Bull's widow had a memorial statue in the shape of an obelisk erected at his birthplace, Ashley Hall, in 1792. Charleston-born architect Robert Mills (1781-1855), who designed the Maxcy Monument in the Horseshoe at South Carolina College in 1827, featured the obelisk memorial to William Bull II in his 1825 map of South Carolina. In 1836, Mills won the design contest for another obelisk, the Washington Monument in the Nation's capital. Mills also designed portions of the Landsford Canal, which began construction in 1820 and ceased operation in 1840. http://www.scencyclopedia.org/sce/entries/bull-william-ii/

http://www.halseymap.com/flash/gov-detail.asp?polID=98

https://south-carolina-plantations.com/charleston/ashley-hall.html#8

https://en.wikipedia.org/wiki/Robert_Mills_(architect)

Secrets in Plain Sight—the 23 part video is a remarkable compilation of ancient history and sacred geometry. http://www.secretsinplainsight.com/

Chapter 9 - Lutheran Theological Southern Seminary

The Labyrinth Society Definition of sacred geometry. https://www.labyrinthsociety.org/sacred-geometry

The Labyrinth Society - To locate a labyrinth, please visit. https://labyrinthsociety.org/

Lauren Artress, author, speaker, and teacher. Founder of Veriditas, World-Wide Labryrinth Project. https://www.laurenartress.com/

LTSS now part of Lenoir-Ryne University of Hickory, NC. https://en.wikipedia.org/wiki/Lutheran_Theological_Southern_Seminary

Chartres Cathedral. https://chartrescathedral.net/

On Peter Champoux's map of these twelve sacred sites, there is a line between Blair, Lake Monticello, and the Lutheran Theological Southern Seminary in the northwest to Middleton Place in the south. What is the connection, you might ask? Could it be the labyrinths at the seminary and Middleton Place?

Chapter 10 - Middleton Place

The Inn at Middleton Place Gardens. https://www.middletonplace.org Call ahead to request access to the labyrinth, which is free to guests staying at the Inn and $5.00 to other visitors.

https://ashleyriverhistoriccorridor.org/sites/

International African American Museum. https://iaamuseum.org/news/

"Building a Place of Pilgrimage" - news story about the new International African American Museum. https://www.postandcourier.com/news/building-a-place-of-pilgrimage-at-charleston-s-international-african/article_226a31be-347d-11e9-bfb5-8f6e468bef5a.html

Chapter 11 - Pearl Fryar's Topiary Garden

Pearl Fryar's Topiary Garden. http://www.pearlfryar.com/

South Carolina Cotton Museum. http://www.sccotton.org/

Chapter 12 - Kalmia Gardens

Kalmia Gardens of Coker College. https://www.kalmiagardens.org/

The triangular-shaped town of Blenheim, SC, named after the Duke of Marlborough's family estate in England, is 34.4 miles northeast of Kalmia Gardens via Hwy 15. The wonderfully unusual Blenheim Ginger Ale was originally created in a building next to the mineral springs and is now produced at the South of the Border complex on I-95. https://scgreatoutdoors.com/park-blenheimmineralsprings.html

http://www.blenheimgingerale.com/about-us/blenheim-history/

Just south of Blenheim lies the hamlet of Parnassus, which comes from the Greek for temple. French botanist Andre Michaux (1746-1805), who brought the first camelias to the Colonies, visited Middleton Place in 1786. He named a local flower Parnassia Caroliniana. http://www.michaux.org/michaux.htm

Following north and almost parallel of Hwy 15 is the famous Hwy 1 that runs from Maine to Florida along a natural geological fault line.

List of Sacred Sites

"Greta Thunberg: They See Us as a Threat Because We Are Making an Impact". https://www.theguardian.com/culture/2019/jul/21/great-thunberg-you-ask-the-questions-see-us-as-a-threat?utm_source=pocket-newtab

Postscript

Dr. Masuro Emoto—author of The Hidden Messages in Water. https://www.simonandschuster.com/authors/Masaru-Emoto/35647842

Sadhguru – The Mystical Secrets of Water. https://www.youtube.com/watch?v=1kKGzCL4D5w

The Sun, Earth, Moon and People: It's All Connected! – Global Coherence Institute/Heart-Math Institute. https://www.heartmath.org/resources/videos/sun-earth-moon-people/

My Uncle Frank, Francis E. Brownell—I believe Frank is sending love and healing to the Congaree Rings. He served at the Battle of First Bull Run. My mother, Jayne Ann Teed Redman, is named after his sister, Jane Ann Brownell Teed. https://en.wikipedia.org/wiki/Francis_E._Brownell

The Congaree Rings

Peter Champoux—Geometry of Place. http://www.geometryofplace.com/serve.html

> *"We shall not cease from exploration*
> *And the end of all our exploring*
> *Will be to arrive where we started*
> *And know the place for the first time."*
> *~ T.S. Eliot (1888-1965)*

Mystical South Carolina: A Pilgrimage to Joy
My Passport to the Twelve Sacred Sites

For information on where to get your passport stamped, please visit www.terileighteed.com

Instructions for My Passport to the Twelve Sacred Sites

When pilgrims walk the Camino de Santiago in Spain, there are places along the route where pilgrims can get their passports stamped. On the Mystical South Carolina pilgrimage route, I make these suggestions for getting your own passport stamped for each sacred site. Each square on your passport represents one of the twelve sacred sites.

Make your own hand-drawn stamp of a happy face, a heart, an angel, your initials, the date, or whatever you choose. Create photographs of the sacred sites, and include a selfie, to remember your visits. Create your own work of art.

Visit a local restaurant, museum, tourism organization, state park, coffee shop, gift shop, bookstore, or other local business and ask to have your passport stamped. For example, visit a restaurant or coffee shop and have a cup of coffee or tea, or a sandwich, and ask your waiter or waitress to initial your passport. Discover new places and meet new friends and have fun!

I would love to hear about your visits to these sacred sites, so please feel free to send me your thoughts and photographs, via my Facebook page https://www.facebook.com/HealingSpiritArt and my website www.terileighteed.com, and by regular mail at P. O. Box 731, Dillsboro, North Carolina 28725. And please subscribe to my newsletter and keep up to date with all the latest news about Mystical South Carolina - A Pilgrimage to Joy.

Blessings and happy journeys to you!

Teri Leigh Teed

About The Author

Teri Leigh Teed is a multidimensional author/artist based in the Blue Ridge Mountains of Western North Carolina near Sylva. Teed's stories and poetry share positive, inspirational, life-affirming thoughts and are part of her "Healing Spirit Art©" portfolio, which includes her award-winning fine art photography.

"Mystical South Carolina – A Pilgrimage to Joy" is Teed's debut book. Inspired by her time and travels while living abroad in London, rural France, and Ireland, and her childhood in her home state of South Carolina, Teed's writings and art reflect her love of Nature and the sacred art of healing.

Teed's photo stories are featured in numerous publications including DailyGood.org and Healing Power of ART & ARTISTS. She is a member of the North Carolina Writers Network and the Academy of American Poets. Her poetry is featured in the Camden Poet's Society 25th Anniversary Collection *What We Keep: Passions of the Heart*, and on TraveleronthePath.com and AscensionGateway.com.

For more information about the author and her work please visit www.terileighteed.com.

NOTES

NOTES

NOTES

NOTES

www.ingramcontent.com/pod-product-compliance
Lightning Source LLC
Chambersburg PA
CBHW060458080526
44584CB00015B/1465